Contents

Any words appearing in the text in bold, **like this**, are explained in the Glossary.

What are kangaroos?

Kangaroos are the only large **mammals** in the world that hop to get around. They have short front legs that they use when walking, but if kangaroos want to move quickly they hop on their large and powerful back legs. Using this bouncing run, the fastest kangaroos can travel up to 31 miles (50 kilometres) an hour and leap 8 metres in each jump!

This is a red kangaroo. Kangaroos have small heads and large ears. Their big feet and large tails help them balance when they run.

What are marsupials?

Kangaroos belong to a special group of mammals called marsupials. All marsupials give birth to young that are only partly developed. The young finish developing in a pouch on the front of their mother's tummy, instead of growing inside their mother like most mammals.

Kinds of kangaroo

There are about 56 different **species** (kinds) of kangaroo in the world. They range in size from tiny musky rat kangaroos that average about 37 centimetres in length to 2-metre tall red kangaroos. There are six large species and these are known as kangaroos and wallaroos. The smaller species are called rat kangaroos, potoroos, tree kangaroos, pademelons and wallabies.

All kangaroos have coats of short hair, which range in colour from white to grey, and from tan to red. In all species the adult **males** are much bigger than the **females** and have more **muscular** chests and arms. Red and grey female kangaroos are known as **flyers**, large males are called **boomers** and young kangaroos are **joeys**.

The musky rat kangaroo is the smallest of all kangaroos. It only weighs about 500 grams and is similar in size to a large guinea pig.

5

Do kangaroos live in groups?

Some species of kangaroos live solitary lives. They spend most of their time alone. They only join other adults to **mate**. Others are more **social** animals. This means that for much of the time they live, feed and stay together in groups and make friendships that last a lifetime. Groups of kangaroos are called mobs.

Red and grey kangaroos

In this book we look mainly at the two largest species of kangaroo – the red kangaroo and the grey kangaroo. Red kangaroos get their name from the males' rust-coloured coat, even though the females have blue-grey hair. Grey kangaroos are grey with white undersides.

This is a group of grey kangaroos. Individual red and grey kangaroos spend some time alone, but most of their lives are spent as part of a group called a mob.

Life in a Mob

Kangaroos

Richard and Louise Spilsbury

www.heinemann.co.uk/library

To order:
☎ Phone 44 (0) 1865 888066
🖹 Send a fax to 44 (0) 1865 314091
🖥 Visit the Heinemann Bookshop at www.heinemann.co.uk/library to browse our catalogue and order online.

First published in Great Britain by Heinemann Library, Halley Court, Jordan Hill, Oxford OX2 8EJ, part of Harcourt Education.
Heinemann is a registered trademark of Harcourt Education Ltd.

Editorial: Nicole Irving and Georga Godwin
Design: Ron Kamen and Celia Floyd
Picture Research: Rebecca Sodergren and Ginny Stroud-Lewis
Production: Viv Hichens

Originated by Dot Gradations Ltd
Printed in China by WKT Company Limited

ISBN 0 431 18269 8 (hardback)
08 07 06 05 04
10 9 8 7 6 5 4 3 2 1

ISBN 0 431 18276 0 (paperback)
09 08 07 06 05
10 9 8 7 6 5 4 3 2 1

British Library Cataloguing in Publication Data

Spilsbury, Richard and Spilsbury, Louise
Animal Groups: Kangaroos – Life in a Mob
599.2'22156

A full catalogue record for this book is available from the British Library.

Acknowledgements

The Publishers would like to thank the following for permission to reproduce photographs:

Ardea/Jean paul Ferrero p. 4; Ardea/John Cancalosi pp. 9, 12; Ardea/P. Morris p. 21; Corbis/Paul A. Souders p.27; Corbis/Theo Allofs p. 22; FLPA/Minden Pictures p. 17; PA/A.N.T p.10; NHPA/Gerard Lacz p. 11; NHPA/Martin Harvey pp. 14, 18, 21, 23; NPL/Dave Watts pp.5, 25, 26; OSF/Adrienne T. Gibson p. 19; OSF/Alan Root p. 16; OSF/Des & Jan Barlett p. 6; OSF/Hans & Judy Beste/AA p. 13; OSF/Stan Osolinski p. 20; OSF/Tony Bomford p. 11; Still Pictures p. 28; Theo Allofs p. 8; TRIP/Australian Picture Library p. 15; TRIP/Eric Smith p. 24.

Cover photograph of the kangaroo mob, reproduced with permission of FLPA/Gerard Lacz.

The Publishers would like to thank Colin Fountain for his assistance in the preparation of this book.

Every effort has been made to contact copyright holders of any material reproduced in this book. Any omissions will be rectified in subsequent printings if notice is given to the Publishers.

What is a kangaroo mob like?

Kangaroo mobs have anything between 2 and 30 members. In a small mob there may be just one adult **male**, two or three **females** with **joeys** and two or three young males. Members of the mob wander off alone or with a few others so you do not often see the whole mob together at the same time. Sometimes several mobs gather together in large groups, especially when food is scarce, such as in times of **drought**.

Living in a mob

One of the advantages of living in a mob is that some kangaroos can act as lookouts while others feed or relax. Kangaroos are especially careful when going for a drink at a **watering hole**. While a mob drinks there will always be one or more guards on duty, keeping a careful eye out for **predators**.

A day in the life of a kangaroo mob ● ● ● ● ● ● ● ● ● ● ● ● ●

In warmer months, the kangaroos in a mob usually spend most of the day resting in a shady spot. At night, when it is cooler, they search large areas for food. In cooler months kangaroos may also feed in the middle of the day and on warm afternoons they may sunbathe.

This is a mob of grey kangaroos in Murramarang National Park, New South Wales, Australia.

Who's who in a mob?

The leader of a mob of kangaroos is the strongest and usually the largest male in the group. He is called the **dominant** kangaroo. He is usually the only male who **mates** with the female kangaroos in the mob. This means that he is the father of all the joeys in the group. As the dominant kangaroo, he also gets the best feeding spots and the shadiest resting-places.

The other male kangaroos in the mob are ranked in importance based on their size, so the smallest male is the least important. Females in the mob look after their young. The older females are dominant over the younger ones. These older females may lead the mob to good places to feed or rest.

This big red kangaroo is known as an old **boomer** or old man – the leader of his mob.

Where do kangaroos live?

Almost all the different **species** of kangaroo live in Australia, but a few live in New Guinea and other islands near by. The grey kangaroo is the only kind of kangaroo that lives on the island of Tasmania.

Different kinds of kangaroo live in different kinds of **habitat**. Some species live just in **deserts** and open **grassland**. Some live on dry rocky hillsides, while others live in forests. Grey kangaroos live in a wide variety of habitats, from high mountain forests to dry open spaces. The red kangaroo lives in Australia's grasslands, **scrublands** (also called 'the **bush**') and hot deserts.

Tree kangaroos

Tree kangaroos live, as their name suggests, in trees. They have longer front legs, are better at walking and have longer, curved claws than other kangaroos. These help them to climb and live in trees.

Many kangaroos live, like these, on dry open lands of northern Australia.

What is a home range?

A **home range** is the area an animal or group of animals travels around to feed, care for young and rest, day to day. Most kangaroo mobs roam over a home range a few kilometres across. The home ranges of different mobs of kangaroos often overlap, but mobs do not try to keep each other out. Kangaroos like to keep to their home range. If they are forced to move away to find food, perhaps during a **drought**, they usually return later.

Rock wallabies are small kangaroos that live in groups on steep rocky hillsides.

Tree kangaroos live in parts of the rainforests of north-east Australia and New Guinea.

11

How do kangaroos cope with the heat?

Most red and grey kangaroos live in habitats that are extremely hot and dry. They live in areas of land where the weather is too hot and dry for trees and many other plants to grow. Instead tough wild grasses take over the land. That is how they got the name 'grasslands'.

Kangaroos have several different ways of keeping cool in their harsh habitat. When they are hopping about quickly, they sweat to help lose some body heat. When they stop, they pant a lot. Panting is when animals breathe quickly to bring in lots of fresh air to cool them down. They may also use their legs to dig into a patch of ground to find cooler earth to lie on.

Kangaroos sometimes lick their own arms to help keep them cool. As the moisture dries in the wind, it takes away some of the heat from their limbs.

What do kangaroos eat?

Kangaroos are **herbivores**, which means they feed on grasses and leaves. Red and grey kangaroos are **grazers** that eat mainly green grass but they will also eat tough, spiny grasses and the leaves of other **bush** plants. The smaller **species** of kangaroo tend to eat leaves, shoots and twigs. The musky rat kangaroo is the odd one out as it is the only kangaroo that eats some meat as well, usually in the form of insects or worms.

Eating on the move

When red and grey kangaroos eat grass they crawl slowly along on all fours, munching as they go. They rest their tails and front paws on the ground and swing their back legs forward to move along. They can use their front paws to push aside shrubs to get at green grass.

Kangaroo mobs spend a lot of time eating. Depending on the season and the amount of food available, they spend between seven and fourteen hours of every day eating.

13

Is grass tough to eat?

The kangaroo's stomach is made up of a set of sacs designed for **digesting** tough, chewy grasses. Like cows, kangaroos also 'chew the cud'. They chew and swallow the tough grass into one part of the stomach. Later they regurgitate it (bring it back into the throat) and chew it again to make it soft enough to digest. Then they swallow this chewed 'cud' into a different part of the stomach for the final stage of digestion.

Where do kangaroos get water?

Like all animals, kangaroos need water to live. Kangaroos get most of their water from the leafy plants that they eat, because these contain a lot of water. They also drink from pools or **watering holes** if they find one. If it is very dry kangaroos may dig pits up to a metre deep to find water.

Kangaroos have very large front teeth for cropping and cutting. The large flat molars further back in their mouths help to grind up their food.

How do kangaroos care for their young?

Red and grey kangaroos usually **mate** in spring or summer. The mother kangaroo gives birth to one **joey** at a time, around a month after mating. The tiny new-born kangaroo then spends between six and eleven months mainly inside its mother's pouch. The father and the rest of the mob help to care for the joey when it comes out of the pouch.

This female kangaroo is ready to give birth. She has licked the pouch clean and then a path in her fur to show the baby the way to the pouch.

Babies inside and out

● ● ● ● ● ● ● ● ● ● ● ● ● ●

Female kangaroos are able to have two joeys developing at the same time. As soon as one baby is born and enters her pouch, the female is able to mate again. The second baby stays inside her body, waiting to be born after the baby in the pouch leaves.

How do baby kangaroos get into the pouch?

When a kangaroo baby is first born it is tiny. It is only 2.5 centimetres long and weighs less than a gram. It is about the size of a small jellybean and it looks nothing like its parents. A new-born kangaroo is completely helpless. It has no hair to keep it warm, it cannot hear and it cannot see. The only things on its little body that have developed are its nose, mouth and its tiny arms.

The new-born kangaroo uses its arms to crawl into its mother's pouch as soon as it has been born. Although it does not have far to go – only about 12 centimetres – this is a dangerous journey. If the baby joey takes too long, the heat of the sun may kill it, or it may die of exhaustion.

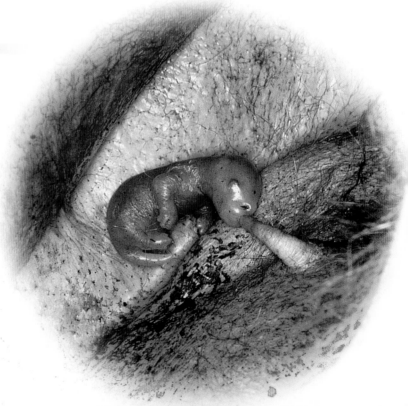

This newly born kangaroo is inside its mother's pouch. It found its way by smelling the trail its mother licked for it.

What happens inside the pouch?

As soon as it is safely inside the pouch, the baby joey chooses one of the four teats there to suckle. As it takes the teat in its mouth, the teat swells up and fills its mouth so the baby stays there and cannot fall off. The joey suckles almost non-stop inside the pouch for up to three or four months. This rich milk helps the baby grow and develop. It grows larger and develops legs, ears, eyes, teeth and hair.

What is suckling?

All **mammal** babies suckle. They drink their mother's milk from teats (or nipples) on her body. Mammal milk is a complete food for babies in the first part of their life, and it even provides all the water they need.

This joey is several months old. It has grown a lot since it arrived in the pouch, but it still needs to suckle for most of its food.

Pouch control

Female kangaroos have muscles that control the pouch. She can close the pouch tight to keep a joey safe inside. If she wants it to leave, she makes the pouch go floppy and tips the baby out!

When does the joey leave the pouch?

From three or four months old the joey pokes its head out of the pouch and starts to learn about life in the mob. A month or so later, it comes out every day to explore. By watching the other kangaroos, joeys learn skills such as where to find food and how to watch out for danger. By ten months old most joeys have left the pouch, although they still stick their head in to suckle until they are a year or more old. By two or three they are adults and can have young themselves.

Up to about a year old joeys still dive headfirst into their mother's pouch for safety or comfort, until she turns them out again!

How do kangaroos relax?

Kangaroos spend the hottest times of the day resting, dozing and chewing the cud. While they are relaxing together like this, members of a mob touch, sniff and **groom** each other. Grooming is when one kangaroo uses its front paws to pick out dead skin, dirt and tiny insect pests (such as fleas) from another's hair to keep them clean. Mother's groom young by licking them and using special grooming claws on their front paws.

Grooming and the mob

Grooming is an important part of a kangaroo mob's **social** life. When animals in a group groom, they end up smelling alike because of the scent in their saliva (spit). It is also a friendly thing to do and makes the animals feel closer to each other. This helps the kangaroos in a mob feel more like a team.

When some kangaroos doze, others in a mob keep a lookout for danger.

Playtime

Young kangaroos spend much of their relaxation time playing. **Joeys** play-fight first with mothers. They return from exploring and before they dive back into the pouch they batter her head and get her to play-fight. Later, joeys play-fight together. When one joey wants to play-fight with another it stands in front of its friend, scratching its sides, as if showing off its **muscular** arms.

When joeys play-fight they grab each other around the neck, touch front paws and kick each other with their back legs. The end of a play-fight is when one pushes another over.

Why do joeys play?

Joeys play for the same reason that young animals all over the world play – for fun. Play also helps young kangaroos get to know the other members of the mob and their place within the group. Play–fighting also helps young **males** to learn good fighting skills because they might need these for real when they are older.

How do kangaroos communicate?

Kangaroo mobs use sounds to **communicate** – to tell each other things. For example, coughs can be a signal from one **male** to tell another he knows it is more **dominant**. Kangaroo mothers make clicking or clucking noises to call their **joeys** to them. When a kangaroo senses danger, it warns others in the mob by thumping its feet on the ground.

When members of a mob hear a kangaroo make a warning thump with its large back feet, they know it has spotted an enemy.

Kangaroos can twist their ears right round to catch the sound of approaching danger or a warning thump from any direction.

21

Do kangaroos from the same mob fight?

Kangaroos in a mob may squabble and push each other over various things such as food or shade, but these squabbles rarely result in real fights. Real fights happen when young **males** challenge the old **boomer** in a mob to try to win the right to **mate** with a **female**.

How does a fight start?

Most challenges begin when one male kangaroo threatens another with various movements called displays. For example, a young male might stand upright and walk towards the other or pull on grass nearby. The old boomer will stand and puff out his chest in reply. Usually these threats are enough for the weaker kangaroo to work out that he would lose a real fight, and he turns and leaves.

The younger male kangaroo in this picture is showing the larger male that he wants to back down from the fight. Old males are so big that young males do not really stand a chance of beating them.

Older and bigger

Most animals, including humans, stop growing when they become adults. Male red and grey kangaroos keep growing taller and stronger throughout their whole lives. Their front arms get bigger and more **muscular** too. Even though the rate of growth slows as they get older, an old male can be more than half as big again as a young adult male.

How do kangaroos fight?

If an old boomer cannot scare off a young challenger, the two will fight. Real fighting is different to play-fighting. Kangaroos try to injure each other by kicking hard in each other's face and stomach using strong legs and sharp claws, and by biting ears. These fights are rare, and most are so one-sided that they end soon after they have begun.

Kangaroos use their front feet to hold their opponent while resting on their tail and giving mighty kicks with their huge and powerful back feet. Adult males often have thicker belly skin that helps protect them.

Does a mob ever change?

Mobs of kangaroos change almost every year. A **boomer** is only the **dominant** member of a mob for about a year. It takes a **male** kangaroo about ten years to grow big and strong enough to win his place as leader. He only manages to remain dominant for a short time because soon someone else wants a turn. When a stronger male challenges the leader to a fight and wins, he becomes the new leader of the mob.

When a dominant male kangaroo has to fight over who leads the mob, he may get badly injured. Old boomers that lose fights against stronger, younger males often die. If they survive, they have to leave the mob and go off to live alone. Most do not survive for very long alone.

Do young kangaroos stay in their mobs?

Most **female** kangaroos stay in the mob they were born in, at least for the first couple of years of their life. Females develop strong bonds with their mothers. Young males usually leave the mob they were born in when new **joeys** are born. These young males often gang together and form new mobs with females from other groups.

What happens when leaders die?

The mob also changes if important kangaroos die or get sick. Some die because of bad weather, when there is flooding or **drought**. Some die in **bush** fires – fires that spread quickly through the dry plants in summer. If older females or dominant males die, other mob members have to fight over which one should take over these important roles.

Drought is when an area of land has little or no rain for a long time. Without water, plants on the land dry up and die. Without plants, kangaroos may starve to death.

What dangers does a mob face?

There are few animal **predators** that can catch and eat large red and grey kangaroos, but there are several that hunt smaller kinds of kangaroos. These include the dingo, a kind of wild dog that lives in Australia, and the wedge-tailed eagle, which attacks **joeys**. In places where houses have been built near wild areas, pet cats and dogs may kill the smaller kangaroos.

Danger and the mob

One big advantage of living in a mob is that kangaroos can watch out for each other. They can take it in turns to look out for danger. When one bangs out a warning with its tail and hops away the whole mob knows to scatter.

This dingo is stalking kangaroos. Big kangaroos will fight off a dingo by kicking if they spot one coming.

Kangaroos and people

Many Australian farmers and landowners think of kangaroos as pests. They hunt or poison kangaroos to get rid of them. They say that red and grey kangaroos jump over fences on to farmland and eat plants meant for their sheep. Some people say that the kangaroos eat different grasses so do not take grass the sheep could eat.

On the road

Members of many kangaroo mobs are knocked down by cars and lorries when they hop at speed across roads. Red and grey kangaroos are very heavy and if a car hits one, both the animal and the people in the car may be seriously injured. Many people who live in the Australian **outback** have a metal grid on the front of their cars to take the brunt of the force in case they collide with a kangaroo. These are called 'kangaroo bars'.

Road warning signs like this one tell drivers where kangaroos might cross. These signs are intended to protect drivers as well as the kangaroos.

What is culling?

In some parts of Australia there are laws that stop people hunting kangaroo mobs. In other areas, people are allowed to shoot a certain number of red and grey kangaroos in order to reduce their numbers. This is called culling. The skin and meat of the animals that are shot are sold. The leathery skins are used to make things such as shoes or footballs, and the meat is sold for people to eat, or to be turned into pet food.

Kangaroos in danger

There are around two million red and grey kangaroos alive today and the **species** is not in danger. However, some of the smaller species of kangaroo, such as the hare wallabies, are **endangered**. They are in danger of becoming **extinct** because people are taking over the land they live on for buildings or farms. Some **conservation** organizations, such as the **WWF**, are working towards protecting these endangered species.

This is a prosperine rock wallaby, one of an endangered kangaroo species.

Kangaroo facts

How did kangaroos get their name?

One story that tells how kangaroos got their name says that when the first European explorers saw kangaroos in Australia, they asked the **Aborigines** what these strange creatures were called. The Aborigines replied, 'Kangaroo', which translates as 'I do not understand your question.' But the explorers thought that was the animal's name!

Life expectancy

In wildlife parks or zoos kangaroos may reach twenty years old, but in the wild most only live for six to eight years. This is because they face many dangers in the wild. Almost half of **joeys** fail to reach two years of age.

Forwards only

The kangaroo's tail is very useful to help it balance when it is hopping, but it is so long and heavy that it makes walking forwards slow and walking backwards impossible!

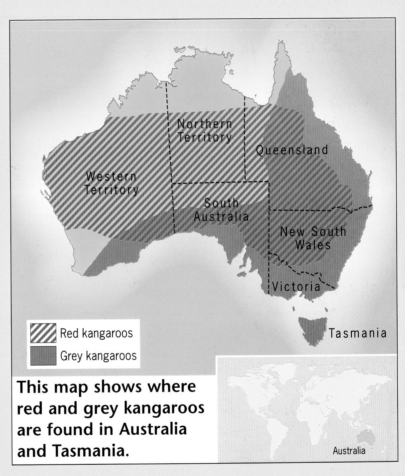

Red kangaroos
Grey kangaroos

This map shows where red and grey kangaroos are found in Australia and Tasmania.

Australia

Can kangaroos swim?

Kangaroos can swim quite well doing a sort of doggy paddle. When they swim, they use their powerful legs and swing their tail from side to side.

Glossary

Aborigines   native Australians. They have lived in Australia for around 40,000 to 60,000 years.

boomers   large male kangaroos

bush   scrubland in Australia

communicate   pass on information

conservation   take action to protect living things and their habitats

deserts   extremely hot and dry places that have short bursts of rain once in a while

digest   what an animal's body does to break down its food and take out the goodness it needs to live and grow

dominant   leader of a group or most important member

drought   when an area of land has little or no rain and the plants there dry up and die

endangered   when an animal or plant species is in danger of becoming extinct

extinct   when there are no members of an animal or plant species left alive

female   animal that, when mature, can become a mother. A female human is called a girl or woman.

flyers   female kangaroos

grassland   areas of land that are mainly covered in grass

grazers   animals that eat growing grass

groom   when one animal cleans bits of dirt, dead skin or insect pests from the hair of another animal

habitat   place where an animal or plant lives

herbivores   animals that eat only or mainly plants and plant parts

home range   area within a habitat that a group of animals lives in

joeys   young kangaroos

male   animal that, when mature, can become a father. A male human is called a boy or a man.

mammal   group of animals that includes humans. All mammals feed their babies milk from their own bodies and have some hair.

marsupials   animals whose babies are carried in a pouch at the front of their mother's body

mate   after a male and female animal have mated, a baby begins to grow inside the female

molars   flat topped back teeth

muscular   full of muscles. Muscles are parts of the body that help to make the bones and the rest of the body move.

outback   wild Australian countryside, far from towns

predators   animals that hunt or catch other animals to eat

scrublands   areas with sandy soil that have patches of trees and lots of slow-growing shrubs

social   living in well-organized groups that work together

species   group of living things that are similar in many ways and can reproduce together

watering hole   place where animals go often to drink water

WWF   world wide conservation organization that is recognized by its panda symbol, and works to protect many animals and their habitats

Find out more

Books

Animals in Order: Kangaroos and Koalas: What They Have in Common, Erin Pembrey (Swan, Franklin Watts, 2000)

Kangaroos and Other Creatures from Down Under, Donald Dale Jackson (Time Life UK, 1979)

Kangaroos and Wallabies, David Watts (New Holland, Australia, 1998)

Life Cycles: The Kangaroo, Sabrina Crewe (Raintree Steck-Vaughn Publishers, 1998)

Life Cycles: The Life Cycle of a Kangaroo, Lisa Trumbauer (Pebble Books/ Capstone Press, 2002)

My World: Kangaroos, Donna Bailey (Heinemann Library, 1996)

Nature Kids: Kangaroos and Wallabies, Pat Slater (Mason Crest Publishers, 2003)

Websites

The WWF has lots of information on kangaroos at www.panda.org

The National Wildlife Federation website will tell you almost all you want to know about kangaroos: www.nwf.org/internationalwildlife/kangaroo.html

Index